GLORY DAYS

WALLACE ARNOLD

ROGER DAVIES & STEPHEN BARBER

AMBERLEY

First published 2007, this edition 2019

Amberley Publishing
The Hill, Stroud
Gloucestershire, GL5 4EP

www.amberley-books.com

British Library Cataloguing in Publication Data.
A catalogue record for this book is available from the British Library.

ISBN 978 1 4456 9463 4 (print)
ISBN 978 1 4456 9464 1 (ebook)

Typeset in 10pt on 13pt Sabon.
Typesetting by Aura Technology and Software Services, India.
Printed in the UK.

Contents

Foreword

"As a bus man who dabbled in coaches, I always used to say buses and coaches are totally different industries. I little realised how true this was until becoming involved in the remarkable story of Wallace Arnold. And if you think it was just a coach operator, read on – you will be amazed at the breadth of the company's interests. It is a fascinating tale and an insight into one of the most high-profile public transport providers in the country." (RD)

"As a coach man, I knew all this. The sheer scale of the Wallace Arnold empire soon dispels any idea that it was just a coach firm from Leeds. And the contribution it made clearly demonstrates the important but unappreciated role coaches play in the UK transport scene. I sometimes worry that I was the last Managing Director of Wallace Arnold, then remember with pride what a privilege it was to work with such a team for one of the country's greatest coach companies." (SB)

But, at its heart. Wallace Arnold was a 'people' firm: strong characters gave it direction and umpteen individuals made it happen. We have tried to bring this personal side into the story to bring alive the memories of a company not long departed. Sit back and enjoy the ride.

Roger Davies,
Stephen Barber,
Oulton Hall,
Leeds,
July 2007

Authors' note

Unless otherwise credited, all pictures are from Stephen Barber's collection and thus form a Wallace Arnold archive. Many of these are from other sources, and we gratefully acknowledge the photographers' efforts in capturing the scenes.

Acknowledgements

Thanks are due to John King, Geoffrey Steel, the late Eric Stockwell, David Braund, Francis Flin, John Flin, John Dodsworth (and for many more tales of coaching!),

In the 1950s and 1960s hiring coaches to the GPO to deliver Christmas mail generated useful extra revenue during the winter months. Pictured in a snowy suburb of Leeds is 1955 AEC Reliance/Burlingham UUG 35, obviously making an express delivery! *J. B. Parkin*

Peter Holt, David Kat, the late Andy Oxley (thanks for the beer, Andy), James Freeman, Alan Millar, Stuart Jones, Gavin Booth, Malcolm Grace, Tony Greaves, Kenneth Evans, Richard Mellor, James Prince, Allan Morse (and all your contacts) and Chris Youhill. Special mention must also be made of the late John Cockshott, who recorded coaching matters at a time when most concentrated on buses.

Publications found useful were Robert Barr's *I Travel the Road*, Stewart J. Brown's definitive history, *Holidays by Coach*, the PSV Circle/Omnibus Society Wallace Arnold fleet history, *Bus and Coach* July 1950, August 1966 and November 1969, *Passenger Transport* March 1968, Brian Parkin's article in *Buses* August 1968, Barry Parsison's article in *Buses* (Annual) '71 and *British Bus Fleets No. 9: Yorkshire Company Operators*.

The Beginnings – Introduction

One day in 1926 a certain Robert Barr handed over £800 to a pair of gentlemen in the bustling Yorkshire city of Leeds to purchase their pioneering charabanc business. This business had become established to the extent that five-day tours to Edinburgh and London and nine-day Scottish Highland tours were being offered by 1922. (The five-day ones cost just over £8 and the Highland one 16 guineas – about £16.80!) The two gentlemen on the receiving end were Messrs Wallace Cunningham and Arnold Crowe, and, strangely, we shall hear little, if anything, further about them. Arnold Crowe took his share and set off in that delightful phrase 'to pursue other interests', but Wallace Cunningham stayed with the new outfit until he died in 1950. Although it seems a little harsh, as I'm sure both were splendid fellows, for the story we are getting into, the decision to market the new acquisition under the old name of Wallace Arnold is perhaps more significant.

But what of Robert Barr himself? If ever the term 'idealist' were appropriate, it is in this man's case. His ideals were, however, backed up by determination and ability. Born in 1889 of Scottish farming folk, he grew up in Woolley, a small village near Wakefield. From here came his deep love for the country, which he described as 'a direct and intense feeling'. He helped his father on the family farm and became, in his words, concerned by the 'hard-working drudgery of farm life'. In the early years of the new century mechanisation was beginning to infiltrate the rural calm, but the young Robert could see its benefits. His father, however, no doubt as a result of a strict Scottish upbringing, was very conservative in his outlook and refused to move with the times. Some machines there were, and Robert was often to be found pulling them to pieces – a task only overshadowed by his not so brilliantly successful attempts at putting them back together again!

High-spots in village life were visits to market, and Robert used to walk through the streets of Wakefield 'and was surprised and disturbed to find people living in such congested surroundings' and having 'no outlook on nature and its beauties'. He remembered fondly his visits to the Yorkshire Dales, notably fishing trips to the Swale, Ure and Ouse, and dreamed of a great experiment to share these delights by taking thousands of city-dwellers to see them.

After one particularly depressing visit, this time to Barnsley, Robert decided that he would leave his beloved countryside and move to the city to become apprenticed in the engineering trade. This was a bold move, as the industry was in its infancy, but Robert saw it as a way to realise his dream. He broached the subject with his mother, who was very upset and shared the view that his father, a very religious Scot, would take a less-than-enthusiastic view of such a departure from generations of farming stock. Robert look a subtle approach, pinning up pictures of motor cars around the home, which his father promptly replaced with ones of horses!

One December afternoon in 1903 Robert took a trip to Leeds – to his eyes an unimaginably huge city – and was offered a job by the proprietor of the Bridge Garage. He could not bring himself to tell his father throughout the following Sunday, so finally, after family worship in the evening, a servant named Rose 'for whom I had a childish reverence' broke the news. True to his principles, his father would not discuss the matter until the following day, and, luckily for all of us, finally agreed. In January 1904 Robert moved into lodgings in Beeston Hill, where he was to stay for 10 years and which, he remarks dryly, 'did as much as anything to crystallise my one ambition to help as many people as possible to get away from the towns into the countryside'.

All this background is necessary to paint the picture of the vision that represented the very small beginnings of the huge empire that became Wallace Arnold. The early days of bus and coach operation are littered with people of vision, and Robert Barr was one of the greatest of them all.

Robert Barr.

The Vision

So how did Robert Barr realise his vision for Wallace Arnold? His wages were dreadfully poor. For the first year they were five shillings (25p) a week, rising by two shillings (10p) per week until the age of twenty-one. However, although cash was short, he had been brought up to be thrifty. He worked overtime, started a cycle-repair business from his digs and was always on the lookout for a deal – something his time in Yorkshire had taught him! By 1912 he had saved a few hundred pounds and bought a Karrier vehicle, which he used around Leeds as a lorry during the week and as a motor coach at weekends. He drove it himself on trips to the old abbeys of Bolton, Rievaulx and Fountains, and he would stop at the roadside and describe the scenery to his passengers.

The dream was becoming a reality, and both lorry and coach fleets grew. But it was only for a short time, for in August 1914 the Great War broke out. Vehicles were requisitioned for war use, and Robert became regional transport co-ordinator for the Ministry of Transport – a role he performed whilst continuing to run what was left of the business. He started afresh after the war and in 1919, with renewed energy, began running further afield. In 1920 he organised his first charabanc trip to London – a remarkable achievement given indifferent road surfaces, solid tyres, a maximum speed limit of 12 mph and a frequent need to stop to top up the radiator with water!

Then came the purchase of Wallace Arnold. The old name of R. Barr (Leeds) was kept for the haulage business, the new name being applied to coaching activities. However visionary, no one could have predicted just how this coach operation would grow into a household name.

Early vehicles were open to the elements, which, of course, limited their use, and it was not long before the Barr fleet started to sport full covers, the first post-war bus, a 1919 Karrier, being fully enclosed. Such modernity was a strong marketing tool. Indeed, in 1921 Wallace Cunningham advertised a five-day tour to the London Motor Show using 'a Super Motor Coach [secured at somewhat heavy cost] absolutely covered in and giving perfect protection no matter what the weather'. By 1928 all fifteen Wallace Arnold vehicles were totally enclosed 'all-weather' vehicles, and from 1927 all new coaches had pneumatic tyres, affording a much-improved ride. This had a further benefit in 1928 when the old speed limit of 12 mph was raised to 20 mph – but for rubber-tyred vehicles only. It was not long before the last solid-tyred vehicles disappeared.

These vehicles operated day tours to the Dales and the seaside, the latter proving so popular that a regular daily coach service leaving Leeds at 9.30am was introduced in the early 1930s. Holiday tours to Devon, Wales and Scotland were also offered.

Vehicles by now were much more reliable, Wallace Arnold having transferred its allegiance to the Lancashire-based company of Leyland Motors for most of its requirements. This reliability gave the company confidence to start Continental tours, the beginnings of a large part of the business, in 1933. The first trips were nine- and 16-day trips to Germany, including a Rhine cruise. It should be borne in mind that in those days coaches had to be lifted on and off cross-Channel ferries by crane, and in 1936 arrangements were made for an operator in Cologne to provide a coach for the Continental leg, thus saving WA this cost and inconvenience.

If this activity doesn't seem too modern, then we tend to think of air travel as something quite recent, but in fact it too was beginning to grow in the 1930s. In a move EasyJet would be proud of, a company called North Eastern Airways began a London–Leeds–Newcastle service. Ever mindful of new trends, WA became its West Yorkshire agent in 1935.

WA built up its presence in the Leeds/Bradford area by acquiring other small businesses, no fewer than fourteen joining the company between 1933 and 1941. This meant that the fleet, which at the beginning of the 1930s had stood at fifteen vehicles, numbered forty by the end of the decade. Where an acquired fleet had built a strong identity WA retained it: a new AEC Regal in 1933 carried the name of Alf Harrison of Leeds, taken over that year, and two new Maudslays of 1936 retained the identity of W. Fish of Morley, a company taken over some three years previously. It was to be a continuing feature of WA policy.

Despite Robert Barr's desire to carry as many city folk as possible, WA tours of the 1930s were run with top-of-the range coaches complete with courier and travelling rugs and stayed at the most exclusive of hotels. They tended to be the preserve of the well-off, and not until after World War II would Robert Barr's original vision be fully realised.

In the meantime the lorry fleet continued to grow, as increasingly more reliable vehicles meant the company could run from Yorkshire to London and over the steep Pennine roads to Lancashire.

A major event in 1937 was Robert Barr's decision to form a public company, the Barr and Wallace Arnold Trust, to take over the transport companies, which at that time comprised R. Barr (Leeds) Ltd, Wallace Arnold Tours Ltd, W. H. Fish & Son Ltd and Alf Harrison (Leeds) Ltd.

During the 1930s many coach firms moved from petrol to diesel engines, as the latter gave greater fuel economy. WA was one of the last to stick with petrol, believing it gave a smoother ride for passengers, its last coaches so powered, some Leyland Tigers, arriving in 1940. They were also the last coaches to arrive before World War II led to the requisitioning of vehicles for the war effort. The remaining coaches did yeoman service providing transport to Royal Ordnance factories and in particular the Avro plant at Yeadon, site of the present-day Leeds/Bradford Airport. To meet these demands, second-hand vehicles were purchased, some surviving to be rebuilt potwar. Significant among the second hand purchases was WA's first double-decker, a Leyland Titan TD1.

Also very significant was the purchase in 1942 of coachbuilder Wilks & Meade, based at Millwright Street, Leeds. This was another farsighted move, the intention being that this firm's coachbuilding skills could be used to rebuild the fleet post-war.

This is precisely what happened, and during the peak years of the late 1940s and early 1950s Wilks & Meade employed more than 250 people. All manner of work was undertaken, including bodies for new coaches, new bodies for some of the ingenious rebuilt chassis WA produced post-war, and bodies for other operators such as Jersey Motor Transport, Sheffield Corporation and Premier Travel of Cambridge, which took some stylish double-decker coaches.

Above: It appears generous grandparents had invited younger members of the family to join them on holiday in Paignton in this delightful 1928 shot. You couldn't want for a better display of fashion of the time! The WA fleet included Leyland, Dennis, Tilling-Stevens and Daimlers at the time.

Left: Drivers Alf Woodhead (left) and Charlie Johnson pose in front of UA 4304, a 1928 Tilling-Stevens B10B (sounds familiar!) with twenty-nine-seat Massey body. In 1933 the coach would be transferred to subsidiary Fish of Morley, lasting until April 1934.

Above: A wonderful example of 1930s marketing.

Below: Why do they always stand in front of the numberplate? A wonderful time-capsule of a 1930s coach holiday, which was very much a middle-class activity; not until the 1950s would coach tours become available to those of more modest means and thus more in line with Robert Barr's original vision.

Above: A typical early-1930s AEC Regal, believed to be EG 9271 of 1934, with thirty-two-seat rear-entrance Burlingham body with roof-mounted luggage rack. Centre entrances were tried in 1935, but in 1936/7 the fleet reverted to rear doors. From 1938 the fleet of half cab coaches standardised on forward entrances.

Below: A majestic line-up of the three 1935 Leyland Tiger TS7s with Burlingham bodywork. They are parked outside the Dunblane Hydro Hotel, much used by WA as its first- or last-night stop on Scottish tours from the North of England – a practice that was to continue well into the 1970s. The chassis of these coaches were to last with WA until 1952, being much rebuilt and rebodied as part of the extensive post-war programme. *The Omnibus Society*

Above: Despite its huge growth, WA always retained close ties with Leeds. Here a Leyland lorry of the R. Barr fleet takes part in a civic parade.

Below: An interesting rear view showing that WA never claimed to be only from Leeds! This lettering was not much changed until the early 1960s. The coaches are both second-hand, UA 8918 of 1929 being purchased in 1941 and FV 5892 of 1935 joining the fleet in 1940. Both were bought to replace vehicles requisitioned for war service but were soon under huge pressure themselves transporting increasing numbers of war workers to factories around Leeds. FV was a Burlingham-bodied Leyland Lion LT7 which was rebodied in 1944 with a bus body from the same firm and again with a Wilks & Meade coach body in 1948, lasting until 1952. UA was another Lion, this time an LTB1 with London Lorries bodywork. *C. W. Tate*

A classic view of the Wilks & Meade product, this 1950 body being mounted on a 1947 Leyland PS1 whose original body had gone onto an older chassis. Looking shiny and new, the coach is seen on tour.

Glory Days (Part One) – Half-Cab Heaven

Post-war austerity made petrol engines uneconomic, and a huge conversion programme involving over fifty coaches was undertaken in the years up to 1950. However, petrol engines were still specified for lighter coaches, mainly Bedfords; these were bought until 1955, the final examples lasting in the fleet until 1959. Further company takeovers were also often dictated by the need for newer vehicles; for example the August 1946 acquisition of Box of Castleford, some way out of traditional WA territory, brought four brand-new AECs, while a Bedford that was on order was delivered direct to the Leeds concern.

If Castleford was a bit out of the way, then the next purchases were a bit of a surprise ... or not, if you look back to WA's early identification of good business to the coast. Four small coach operators in Scarborough were bought in 1945, bringing with them four coaches, but, correctly anticipating huge demand for a seaside break after six years of war, WA allocated twelve new Bedford OBs to the resort's fleet in 1947. Initially using one of the acquired names, Barker's, the fleet adopted full WA identity in 1949.

All this was very fine, but you get the feeling that Robert Barr's first love was the coach tour. It seemed best to fit his ideal of introducing people to the countryside. During the 1930s coach design had come on in leaps and bounds, prompting Robert to remark: 'By the time the outbreak of war put a stop to pleasure travelling, motor coaches had ushered in a new era of safe, speedy and reliable travel.' He stated that their patrons were now able to travel in comfort unimaginable in days gone by and made the delightful comparison of this 'kingdom of the road' with the monotonous swiftness of trains. He even quoted Ruskin: 'Railway travelling is not travelling at all, it is merely being sent to a place and very little different from becoming a parcel'. Of all the tour destinations served by WA, one stands out as a particular favourite and was one of the most popular – Devon. In 1945 this interest was given substance by the purchase of two connected hotels in Torquay, the Trecarn and Oswalds.

It is perhaps less surprising in this context that in 1947 WA purchased a typical seaside excursion operator, Waverley's of Paignton. Four new OBs were despatched south but retained the Waverley name. Ruby's of Paignton was bought in 1949; again the name was kept, but in due course a joint brochure, referring on the back to being 'associated with Wallace Arnold Tours', was produced.

Post-war, demand for leisure travel was huge as folk shook off the restrictions of wartime and took refuge from what were still very austere times. The bus and coach industry struggled to meet this demand, and the requirement for new vehicles was overwhelming. WA overcame this as best it could by rebuilding pre-war vehicles and purchasing as many new ones as possible. Between 1946 and 1950 it bought new forty-eight Leyland Tigers, eleven having the new, larger (8-litre) engine, which was more difficult for the engineers to work on, as they were taller to lift off the engine block. Also new were thirty-four Bedford OBs, twenty-four AECs, ten Daimlers and one Guy, all these seating between twenty-nine and thirty-three passengers. Bodywork mainly came from three suppliers – Duple, Burlingham and, of course, Wilks & Meade, which provided no fewer than forty vehicles. The purchase of ten further coach operators in the Leeds and Scarborough areas in 1945/6 brought with them a further twenty assorted vehicles.

To service this demand WA had opened up booking offices in ten northern towns, plus one in London, to which we will return. Additionally arrangements were made for agencies in twenty-three other towns, sometimes with other operators, such as Hall Bros in South Shields, or in Leeds, Hull, Sheffield and York with the Thomas Cook travel business. Tour departures from Leeds, Scarborough, Bridlington and Hull rose to twenty-one a week, while ten days could be had in Devon and Cornwall for £19.50. As soon as possible express services to the coast were reintroduced, at first daily from Leeds to Blackpool but soon joined by daily summer services to Bridlington, Filey, Scarborough and Southport. £51 would buy you fourteen days in Switzerland, at first the only Continental destination but joined in 1949 by the French and Italian rivieras and the Netherlands. This last, being flat, was served by Bedford OBs!

In April 1946 WA first opened its bookings for holiday express services. Six years of war, continuing austerity and the fears over availability gave rise to never-to-be-repeated scenes such as this outside Leeds Corn Exchange.

Above: The Calls in the late 1940s with two Duple Leyland TS8s, on the right HUA 904 of 1939 and on the left JUA 374 of 1940. Both vehicles would later be subjected to body transfers, rebuilding and re-engining.

Below: A splendid line-up further along The Calls in the late 1940s. Most of these coaches would later be rebuilt with full fronts and painted in the all-cream livery.

Above: LNW 86, a Daimler with Wilks & Meade body. In 1952 it received a Burlingham body with a Plaxton full front from a Leyland PS2 (NUA 752); then in 1957 it received a double-deck Roe body, the coach body going to Regal MUA 497. In the background is HG 7118, a 1939 AEC Regal/Burlingham formerly with Morecambe Motors.

Below: The driver of HE 7122, a 1936 Leyland TS7 with a much-rebuilt Duple body, has a chat with a fellow driver leaning nonchalantly against a convenient corner. Perhaps he is on a spare duty and has an overnight case packed.

Above: Starting-handle to the fore, GUA 829, a 1938 Leyland TS8 with a Duple body rebuilt by Wilks & Meade, reverses into a parking place. It makes you wonder how folks found the right coach!

Right: KUA 14, a 1946 Leyland PS1 with Wilks & Meade body.

MUM 275 stops in Wharf Street, Leeds, whilst the full load of passengers wonders if their driver is going to talk to his mate long enough for a quick visit to the Normandy Cafe. The coach is a 1949 Daimler CVD6 with thirty-three-seat Wilks & Meade body. In 1956 it would receive a double-deck Roe body.

Above: Typical Scarborough fare until the 1960s was the classic Bedford OB/ Duple combination, something most people refer to simply as a Bedford/Duple. Doesn't this just sum up summer excursions in the 1950s? GWX 74 stands at the Harbourside pick-up point, rented from the local council, about to do a trip to Oliver's Mount for 6p at today's money. *R. F. Mack*

Below: A postcard produced in-house for holidaymakers in Torquay to send to friends – after a splendid day out, no doubt. Despite the reference to Waverley Tours – a firm taken over in 1947 – the coach was pure WA, a Wilks & Meade-bodied Leyland PS1.

A Capital Idea

WA was very mindful of the potential offered by the South East, particularly London and its tourist market. Many Americans had learned about the city during war service, and there was a strong business in return visits during peacetime. In 1948 WA took the bold step of purchasing Homeland Tours of Croydon. This company, set up by Francis Flin, had originally run from Croydon and King's Cross to Thanet but after the 1930 Act had had a run-in with the East Kent Road Car Co. The latter lost, but in 1935 Homeland's overdraft was called in, so the business was sold to East Kent. In 1936 tour licences of the local Wilson's Tours were bought, and a programme of high-quality tours using Leyland Tigers down-seated to twenty-two was introduced the following year. The business broke even in 1938, but the outbreak of war in 1939 stopped development. The fleet had wheels removed, was mounted on bricks and hidden in a Wiltshire barn, to avoid requisitioning! After the war two coaches were put back on the road, but the shortage of new coaches prevented the business starting up properly. A chance meeting between Francis and Robert Barr in 1947 resulted in WA's buying the licences, Homelands taking on its first WA operations in 1948. Francis, son of the founder, recalls that terms were agreed by phone, charts and brochures turned up and they just got on with it – no formal agreement existed throughout Robert Barr's time! Tours picked up in the municipal car park in Croydon and King's Cross coach station, access to the Yorkshire programme being provided by means of a train from London. Trains were also used to feed into Croydon. The American market was particularly targeted, brochures being produced with US dollar prices, a fourteen-day Scottish tour in 1949 costing $190. All the work was planned in Leeds, Homeland's becoming the administration and booking centre as the business grew. Coaches were parked and washed at Crystal Palace football ground, and drivers' digs were located in that area. Emergency coach repairs were carried out by Coneyhall Garage, a local Rootes dealer owned by the Flins. As WA coaches were away by 09.30 this was a largely unknown part of the company's operation, although when coach terminal facilities were in short supply in the 1960s one operator was heard to remark that King's Cross wasn't an option as it was 'half-full of Wallace Arnolds'! It wasn't unknown to customers though; indeed, in 1970 no fewer than 141 tours were operated from London. This was comparable with the total from Yorkshire, and, at its peak, WA carried more passengers from the South than the North! Robert Barr certainly saw an opportunity in Croydon.

These challenging and exciting times were overshadowed by the threat of Nationalisation. In the 1948 annual report Robert Barr wrote: 'I myself feel that no advantage would accrue to anyone by a business such as this being nationalised in any form; it is essentially personal business involving a great deal of personal effort in arranging routes and hotels and so on and does not form an essential part of the basic transport services of any district.' The threat moved away from the passenger business, not to arise again until 1968. However, R. Barr (Leeds) Ltd, the lorry side, was nationalised in 1949, becoming part of British Road Services.

In the 1950s things began to get tough for the industry. Costs began to rise, and the growth of car ownership began changing the environment in which coaches and buses ran. This was not lost on successive Governments, which soon came to regard taxation on fuel as a golden goose and merrily slaughtered it for all their worth. In the two years up to 1952 tax increased from 20 per cent of the price of a gallon to more than 60 per cent. Drastic measures were needed.

Left: Seen just prior to nationalisation, this is a classic post-war ERF flatbed lorry in the R. Barr fleet.

Below: Despite being in Leeds, WA always used its newest coaches on London departures, as seen in the three views between 1958 and 1962 at King's Cross coach station on Pentonville Road. Just look at the magnificent glazed roof on Plaxton-bodied 8333 U (and ponder how much it registration would fetch today). Leopard 67 BUA possibly took the rounded-front concept a bit too far! *Stephen Barber Collection; D. F. Parker; Geoff Stainthorpe*

A Revolution, Under the Floor

During the war years the BMMO ('Midland Red') company in Birmingham, which built its own buses, had devised a new type of single-decker with the engine under the floor. Coupled with successive increases in length and width, this allowed a coach to carry up to forty-one passengers, so that two new vehicles could carry the load of three old ones. Mainstream manufacturers, urged on by the industry, were quick to follow this lead, and by 1951 underfloor-engined vehicles were appearing in increasing numbers. WA was quick to take advantage of this, and in that year ten of Leyland's Royal Tiger and three of AEC's Regal IV entered service. But it wasn't just the size; the new engine position allowed the coach to be fully fronted, incorporating either a front door or an extra pair of seats, which must have given the most splendid view on the road! Coachbuilders leaped to the challenge, introducing stunning new styles. Not all worked, but WA's were examples of one of the most successful, the Burlingham Seagull.

Overnight, front-engined coaches became obsolete. In a business where looks mattered a great deal this took something of the gloss off the new coaches. WA launched into a massive programme of rebodying or rebuilding, one of the largest in the industry, even cascading bodies to older chassis and mounting new full-fronted bodies on the newer front-engined chassis to disguise their age. This made them heavier and less easy to work on, but what the heck? They looked modern! In total, from 1946 until 1954 no fewer than 116 coaches were involved in this programme, Wilks & Meade being fully involved in the task. The last half-cabs, some AEC Regals taken over with the Box business, went in 1955.

The last front-engined coaches were delivered in 1950 and, anticipating the trend, had been fitted from new with full-fronted bodies. They also dropped the red trim, adopting a livery of all-over cream. Notable amongst these and fitting in with the desire to tap into the American market was Leyland Tiger NUG 1, which was luxuriously appointed with 2+1 seating for 21 (in lieu of the usual 33) and glazed sliding roof panels. It was duly shipped across the Atlantic to appear, in a blaze of publicity, at the 1950 British Automotive Exhibition in New York (sometimes referred to erroneously as the World Fair).

It soon became clear that the new underfloor-engined types were not without their problems. The Royal Tiger, in common with many of the breed, had an alarming reluctance to stop – a trait eased later by the fitting of air brakes. A solitary Sentinel that entered service in 1955 had the same problem. Perhaps of more concern was the increase in weight – almost a ton a coach – and it was not long before manufacturers were trying feverishly to shed weight. The results, in 1954, were the Leyland Tiger Cub and the AEC Reliance. WA tried them both, finding the Albion-produced two-speed axle on the Leyland unsatisfactory (and unpopular with drivers) but considering the excellent synchromesh on the AEC the best of its kind, and for the rest of the decade the Reliance dominated orders. The good news was that both types achieved remarkable fuel economy, returning more than 15 mpg on tour work. Quite an achievement!

There was, however, still room at the lighter end of the market. This was Bedford's fiefdom, but in the 1950s it was challenged. One of the first off the block was Commer with its Avenger series, and between 1954 and 1957 WA took seventeen of the type, many going to Devon. Diesel they may have been but their front-mounted two-stroke engines were noisy, and they proved unpopular. Bedford also came up with a diesel, WA buying one in 1959 along with another challenger, a Ford Thames 570E, for comparison. Perhaps more important and certainly more significant was that the Ford and three other new coaches for 1959 were leased from the well-known dealership, Stanley Hughes of Cleckheaton. WA had hired second-hand coaches before, but the application of this to new coaches was truly revolutionary for the industry and indicative of WA innovation. It was to become a major part of the company's vehicle policy from this point on.

Until the mid-1960s the Leeds coach fleet was based at Hunslet Road, one of the city's main arteries and also associated with railway-locomotive manufacture. The site included depots, workshop and off-street parking facilities. AEC Regal III MUA 497 was a classic example of the amazing rebuilding, rebodying and body-swapping that went on in the late 1940s and early 1950s: new in 1949 with a twenty-five-seat Duple body, it was first reseated to thirty-three, then rebuilt with a full front by Yeates in 1952; in 1956 it received (from Daimler LNW 869) the J950 Burlingham body, seen here, which had originally graced Leyland PS2 NUA752 and had gained this Plaxton full front!

Above: What can you say? The ultimate atmospheric shot, recorded inside Burlingham's Blackpool factory in 1951. Indicative of the huge leap in design brought about by underfloor-engined chassis, WA's Royal Tiger OUB 76 contrasts with the North Western Bristol L on the left of the picture. Lurking in the background are some double-deckers for local Blackpool Corporation to a streamlined design introduced before the war. BCT might reasonably claim that, at last, design had caught up with it!

Below: At the Harbourside pick-up point in Scarborough, two fine heavyweight specimens on layover during private-hire duties from Leeds in May 1953. It is interesting to note how with the same remit, Duple (on AEC Regal IV 479) made such an uninspiring attempt on the new underfloor-engined chassis, whilst Burlingham (Leyland Royal Tiger 289) managed such a classic. The local depot never had anything as grand as this, the fleet being based on the Bedford OB. *D. Akrigg*

More 'nothing new under the sun': Continental exit on 1957 Reliance/Burlingham YUM 56.

Boom Time

Despite growing car ownership, demand for coach tours and holidays boomed in the 1950s. Licensing by the Traffic Commissioners saw to it that there were strict regulations on routes, fares and vehicle numbers on all services, but WA nevertheless faced stiff competition. In Leeds it was challenged by Heaps Tours and state-owned West Yorkshire Road Car. In Bradford, so numerous were the operators vying for the key city-centre pick-ups alongside the Alhambra Theatre that slots were allocated every day by a straw-poll. Each operator took turns in administrating the poll, and it is notable that WA seemed to be responsible for the busiest days and seemed to get the prime slots at the head of the queue! After the 1955 acquisition of major competitor Feather's Tours, with its very modern fleet, this trend seemed even more pronounced! WA kept the Feather Bros livery of blue and silver for more than ten years. In addition to city-centre sites both Leeds and Bradford had a large number of suburban picking-up points. It is difficult to remember just what restrictions the old licensing system placed upon routes, pick-ups, fares and frequencies. All applications were open to objection, and public inquiries would be held to decide the matter. Often the purchase of a company was as much for its licences as anything else, and this is a major part of our tale, to which we will return. As an example, WA was keen to become established in Lancashire, but objections from the myriad of local operators had prevented this happening. Then, in 1954, WA bought the tour licences of the Yelloway Company, based in Rochdale. Many had been dormant for some time, and each application for renewal brought a storm of objections, at times resulting in public inquiries lasting seven or eight days! Quietly, in 1958, WA gave up.

Things were much more successful in Scarborough. Early in 1952 Hardwick's was purchased, giving many more excursion licences in the town. For example, a trip to Oliver's Mount was on offer for 1/3d (today a remarkable 6p!). But the purchase also brought something new – a bus route to Ebberston. So good was this that WA not only kept it on but also invested in it the very first new double-decker ever bought, an all-Leyland PD2 in 1953. A similar machine was added the next year. The Hardwick's name would be retained until 1987, when it was sold to East Yorkshire Motor Services.

Later in 1952 the bus-operating side expanded further with the purchase of the Farsley Omnibus Co., based in Stunningly, west of Leeds; this ran buses between Pudsey and Horsforth and by 1959 was carrying 2.3 million passengers a year. And, finally, in 1956, local bus operation was further expanded, this time east of Leeds with the purchase of the Kippax & District fleet of six buses running from the city to Garforth, Kippax and Ledston Luck. By 1959 this operation was carrying 1.4 million passengers a year.

But it was the coaching side that was the main part of the business. In 1954 tours started to the Republic of Ireland and to Northern Ireland, the brochures still showing prices in pounds sterling and $US. By 1955 the company was carrying 25,000 tour passengers a year.

However successful the company's main business, the Trust was becoming increasingly concerned by the threat posed by the demand for personal transport, and in another bold move it decided to enter the world of vehicle dealership. At first it hitched its wagon to the fading Sentinel business, even putting one of that builder's coaches in service, but it soon learned enough to arrange a franchise agreement with the Nuffield Group, representing such well-known names as MG, Morris and Wolseley. One day in 1958 the Chairman of Associated Commercial Vehicles, Lord Brabazon of Tara, opened Wallace Arnold Sales & Service's 100,000 sq. foot car salesroom in Hunslet Road, with some of the largest plate-glass windows in Leeds. The Wilks & Meade business was amalgamated with the dealership to bring bodywork expertise.

The coach side was not neglected, and in the late 1950s, following the purchase of three operators in Torquay, operations in the West Country were consolidated under the Wallace Arnold (Devon) identity. But it is to Leeds again that we must turn for a major development. In 1957 a new coach station, which daily turned into a carpark after the departure of coaches, was opened in The Calls, on the edge of the city centre (and nowadays home to some really rather swanky hotels and restaurants). WA earned praise from the Traffic Commissioners for its efforts to avoid city-centre congestion caused by coaches picking up passengers. Express services grew dramatically throughout the 1950s, Blackpool and the 'SFB' (Scarborough, Filey, Bridlington) being cornerstones. Timings on these services were dictated by seaside landladies, outbound passengers being able to take over their rooms whilst homecoming folk, evicted for cleaning to take place, sat on their cases, waiting for the coach home! Other services linked Leeds with Morecambe, Paignton, Skegness, Torquay and Southport. Particularly significant was the daily service from Leeds, Bradford and Huddersfield to Ringway Airport in Manchester. Here we need to embrace another WA feature. The top-line services, holiday tours and suchlike, were always covered using WA vehicles. For everything else, if a WA vehicle were not available coaches were hired in. And WA took no prisoners! John Dodsworth, of Dodsworth Coaches, remembers well what hired operators had to endure: "You'd go off to the self-catering holiday camps on the East Coast, carrying folks with huge cases full of food," he recalls. Sometimes, snarling dogs would make ticket-checking impossible, until WA banned dogs! But it was the Ringways he remembers most. WA timed them as tight as possible, and, with no motorway, travel over the Pennines, stuck behind a crawling lorry, could be painfully slow. Driving fast to make up time to connect with planes was par for the course. Ringway then was but a few sheds near the planes, and coaches would drive up to them through a narrow gateway. At each side of the gate was a fire bucket full of water to throw over the red-hot brake drums of the arriving coaches. "Only did it on the nearside, steam everywhere, so the passengers didn't get burned getting off," remembers John, "and your last job before leaving was to top up the buckets!" Even more nerve-wracking in those pre-motorway days was getting to Bournemouth's Hurn

Airport for Channel Islands flights. Stephen Barber remembers trying to soothe the Air Traffic Controllers over a late-running coach, finally being put through direct to the captain on the aircraft's flight-deck to assure him that his passengers would be arriving soon!

The whole express-service operation claimed to cover 300,000 miles and carry 80,000 passengers in 1959. Expansion came by acquisition too and, in total in the 1950s, WA bought eleven other operators. The last one, in January 1959, was the modern eleven-coach operator, Kitchen's of Pudsey, right in the company's heartland.

It is interesting to note that, even in early-post-war days, coach operators saw the different market offered by elderly people. In 1955 WA became one of the first coach operators to offer cheaper off-season coach tours for older folks, even starting a savings club whereby stamps in various denominations could be bought to pay for them. This was part of the company that was to grow hugely. All manner of ideas were tried. One year, in order to keep prices down, B&Bs were used instead of hotels, each coach using three or four different establishments. It was a disaster! Each morning the coach would collect its charges, who would then immediately compare breakfasts. "We had two fried eggs!" "Well, we had three, so there!"

At the other end of the scale WA caused a bit of a stir in 1961 by running a coach tour 4,214 miles from Leeds to Moscow and back. At the height of the Cold War this was quite a feat, and it was not to be repeated for twenty years. This was not the plan, however. When Malcolm Barr – Robert's son, by now Assistant Managing Director – and his daughter, Tours Director Mrs Margaret Hook, flew to Moscow in September 1960, seventeen- and eighteen-day tours and educational visits for children were envisaged. It is another example of WA's pioneering spirit – and also a willingness to accept when things don't turn out exactly as expected. Driver Jack Marsay duly pointed 9907 UG – a 'super-powered' Plaxton-bodied Leopard complete with £200 of spares, facilities to brew up and a kitchen sink for washing up – out of The Calls on 17 June 1961 and headed towards Moscow. An interpreter, Bill Gibson, was on board, as was *Yorkshire Evening Post* reporter Barrie Farnhill, who sent back regular reports. Barrie was no stranger to things road transport and wrote pieces about them in the *Post* on a regular basis; indeed, in February 1960 he penned an article about travelling to Rome by service bus. Whether this gave WA initial ideas about such a service on a more direct basis we'll never know, but there is no doubt that WA got a fair amount of good publicity in the local press. A sound investment. The Moscow coach travelled out via Ostend, Aachen, Nuremberg, Prague, Brno, Lvov, Kiev, Kharkov and Kursk. After three days in Moscow it returned via Smolensk, Minsk, Warsaw, Poznan, Berlin and Hanover, crossing back to Harwich. The twenty passengers, average age fifty-five, were warned by Bill that in many ways the trip was a 'journey into the unknown'. Barrie cheerfully reported that no one had the faintest idea where they were going to stay in the Soviet Union; this was in the hands of the Intourist guide due to join the coach at the border. Replete with steak and chips and armed with chewing gum as gifts for Soviet children, our plucky band set off. Their aim was to see how the Russian man in the street fared, and Bill, who had been doing this sort of thing for forty years, assured everyone that said person, proud that he was being visited, would be friendly and anxious to help. Mr B. Foster, a chemist from Hull, wanted to see how Russia had changed since he visited it before the war, while a couple just returned from a world cruise could not resist the lure of Moscow. Mr H. E. Cook from Horsforth just wanted 'to see for himself'. Barrie leaves us with the engaging picture of phrase books coming out, noting that 'the air was shrill with tortured grunts and whistles as Anglo-Saxon tongues grappled wildly with West Riding-style Russian'.

It must all have been too much, as it wasn't repeated, but what a bold move! Also, the weather improved in 1961 (after a dire 1960), and record numbers of passengers were carried on the company's tours, not only from Leeds but also incoming through London, so the hassle of Iron Curtain travel was probably considered unnecessary. In any case, by 1962 WA could boast that it offered holidays from Orkney to Ibiza, the foreign programme including Norway and holidays by rail and air.

Sadly the exciting events of the summer of 1961 were overshadowed by the death, at the age of seventy-one, of Robert Barr. His funeral, at Leeds Parish Church, was attended by mourners from the local business community, the industry and many from the company. Robert was a mighty presence over WA. A favourite saying of his was: "If the daily orders aren't done, tomorrow cannot happen". Geoffrey Steel, the company's Licensing Officer at the time, recalls one of the regular occasions when Robert took 100 seats at the Grand Theatre, Leeds, to treat staff to a show; things were looking a bit wobbly for the morning, so at the 9 pm interval Geoffrey and his assistant, Richard Verity, slipped out to the office to make sure that everything was covered! Following Robert's death his son, Malcolm, took over the role of Chairman.

Reliance/Plaxton 9197 NW of 1959 shows off well the attractive blue and silver livery inherited with the purchase of Feather Bros in 1955 and retained by WA until 1962.

Above: After the purchase of Hardwick's in 1952 WA felt the bus route was strong enough to invest in and bought two new all-Leyland PD2s in 1953/4. The second of these classic machines is seen passing the West Yorkshire depot at Northway in the days when buses had the roads to themselves.

Below: One of the buses taken over with Farsley Omnibus, numbered 9 in that fleet, was this thirty-five-seater Roe-bodied Daimler CVD6 of 1948. It is seen in typical surroundings in the village of Farsley, at a location still recognisable today.

Above: Not blessed with the most elegant of Plaxton bodies, Leopard 833 KUA helps out on Tours from Bradford on a busy Saturday, still displaying its Farsley Omnibus destinations!

Below: Eleven coaches bought in 1956 tried front entrances and had flat screens on their Burlingham bodies, to reduce replacement costs. Some (one fitted with seats from a Rotherham Trolleybus!) ended up on bus work, including Leyland Royal Tiger WUM 49, seen near Leeds bus station in the employ of Farsley Omnibus. It is followed by a West Riding Guy Wulfrunian, a type pioneered by this operator. Despite many revolutionary features, these things were a bit of a disaster and brought down Guy Motors. Its red colours in a green-liveried fleet denoted working on a former tram route.

Above: Kippax was the busiest and most profitable bus route and justified the use of 30-foot seventy-three-seater Leyland PD3s with the refinement of platform doors. Bodywork, by Roe, was built nearby at Cross Gates, Leeds.

Below: The date is 16 August 1958, and Reliance/Duple WUM 44 is loading passengers for its Blackpool express at a site near The Calls. Come on, cheer up – you're on your holidays!

Above: It may be August – 16 August 1958, to be precise – but this lady, no doubt waiting for her husband to "just pick up a paper, love", is taking no chances with the weather. The driver in long white coat chats with some of his passengers beneath typical advertisements of the time, (Today £3 a day to park in central Leeds is cheap!) Reliance/Burlingham TNW 23 waits to set off for the Cornish Riviera ... as soon as the paper comes.

Below: "Wish I'd thought t'bring hat like that – can't tell if weather will be reet all day!" These gentlemen, about to set off in August 1958, probably have no idea that, eight years previously, their steed had graced the streets of New York. Mind you, it was shorter and had a different body then!

Above: Saturday in August 1964, and the 'SFB' (Scarborough, Filey, Bridlington) expresses are loading. Two WAs lead the way including this Duple-bodied Ford. There were numerous drop-off points, as the windscreen stickers reveal, and loading the huge numbers of people onto the right coaches was an art!

Below: It's 08.00 on a Saturday morning in the early 1960s, and loading of the Morecambe express service is underway. Look at the orderly queue being formed! Use of hired coaches was standard practice at weekends, and the 'On Hire To Wallace Arnold' sticker can be seen on the nearside windscreen of this Bedford SB/Duple.

Above: Weekend troop services were common in the 1950s during the time of conscription, offering home leave to troops based mainly in the South of England. WA made extensive use of other operators' coaches on hire; arriving in northern cities late on Friday and not departing until Sunday, they were available for use on Saturday. Silver Star of Porton Down, near Salisbury, was a famous name in such operations and ran weekly to Leeds. Here its 13, an all-Leyland Royal Tiger, takes a break on a WA express halfway between Leeds and Southport.

Below: Bradford's Morley Street was used by all licensed excursion operators in the city. Consolidation meant that WA held the majority of licences. This Yeates-bodied Bedford of Kitchins Tours, with a traditional chalkboard being used to tout for business to Kilnsey Show in September 1962, had been bought along with the business by WA in 1959, it is seen outside the office of Feather Bros, a WA subsidiary since 1955. The Kitchin name would be retained until the late 1960s.

Above: Kitchins purchased two of these Reliance/Plaxtons in 1958, the year before the firm was taken over by WA, with which they were to last until 1967. One of WA's Reliances of the same age, but with a very different Plaxton Consort body, is seen behind UWY 666 in this April 1958 view; obviously WA had slipped up! It's a long time since Seaburn was an excursion destination.

Below: WA tour coaches often started in Bradford before journeying to Leeds for the majority of their customers. Here, on 26 May 1961, a 1959 AEC Reliance/Plaxton Panorama prepares to depart for Rothesay. Sadly WA subsequently decided against this modern design, sticking with centre entrances and sliding windows for many years to come.

Above: A new Ford/Duple in Kitchins red and grey seeks custom for a half-day tour to Saltburn on a damp April Fool's Day 1961. Licensing restrictions dictated that a half-day tour could not depart before 12:00!

Below: The Kitchins livery was adapted in 1962 for the Feather Bros fleet, as demonstrated by a nearly new Plaxton-bodied Bedford VAL preparing to leave for a tour to Paignton in June 1965. Note the WA symbol in the fleetname and the remarkable contrast with the Reliance behind from the same bodybuilder. What are the couple up to in the entrance to the Alhambra?

Above: In 1960 Wardways of Bingley – near enough to Bradford to be part of its magnificent trolleybus system – was taken over. Its ten coaches were immediately sold, but the fleetname was retained, albeit in house style, as shown on this new Bedford VAL in May 1966.

Below: Coach tours to Russia held great attraction for the company, but during the Cold War it was difficult. In 1961 WA managed it, and here Robert Barr, on the extreme right, poses with the intrepid travellers outside Leeds Corn Exchange on their way to Moscow. Their apparel is more suited to a week in Eastbourne, even in the comfort of the relatively sophisticated Leopard coach! It was not until the Gorbachev years that WA coaches reached Moscow in any numbers, and from the late 1980s the 'Grand Russian Spectacular' became one of the company's most popular European tours, three coaches often being required on each departure.

WA always associated itself with local sporting teams and their supporters. For much of the company's existence Leeds United was a prestigious club, and WA provided the team coach. In this fabulous scene, full of the atmosphere of the mid-1950s, an AEC Reliance/Burlingham takes LUFC supporters past the site that was to become Gelderd Road depot. Note the flying squad on the left...

Above: A contract was held with the Tote Board to take staff to racecourses. A 1959 Reliance/Plaxton is seen at Ripon Races in July 1965.

Below: The Leeds United team arriving for a civic reception in their home city in 1965, having come second in the FA Cup Final. Anyone recalling the Revie era will recognise the players sticking out through the roof.

How Fares the Fleet?

But what of the vehicles of the time? The initial Ford T obviously made a good impression, no fewer than forty-seven entering service between 1960 and 1963 against only ten Bedfords. After that the balance went the other way. As was now normal WA practice, there was a mixture of purchases and hirings. A major shift took place in the heavyweight fleet as well. In 1959, to replace the Tiger Cub, Leyland introduced its more powerful Leopard, and WA took one of the first examples. Such was the success of the Leopard that, with the exception of 1966, Leylands outnumbered AECs throughout the 1960s.

Vehicle dimensions too experienced a major change. In 1961 the regulations were changed to increase the maximum permitted length of coaches to 36 feet, allowing forty-nine seats.

WA was quick to take advantage, standardising on this length and capacity for heavyweight vehicles, which were generally kept for eight years. The lightweight day-excursion fleet still standardised on forty-one seats, and shorter, narrower coaches continued to be specified for Devon operations, to fit the narrow roads used. A feature of the bigger coaches was the continued use of centre entrances, something introduced with underfloor-engined coaches but by now quite rare. The last centre-entrance coaches entered the fleet in 1967 and would last until 1977. Bedford and Ford responded to the new length with new models, in the latter's case the 676E, not the happiest of coaches. Bedford took a different line introducing the VAL, a chassis with two front steering axles. Despite being hard on tyres and brake linings the arrangement gave a smooth ride, and VALs featured in the fleet intake from 1963 until 1969.

But perhaps the most striking impact on the fleet came in 1968. A new livery designed by Ogle adorned Leopard/Plaxton thirty-seat executive coach MNW 335F. The livery was of grey and white with a bold new orange WA logo on the side, the design criterion having been to make the background dull so that the logo stood out. Somehow, it was just too dull, and a chance remark by a member of staff resulted in the application of orange wheels that set the whole thing off perfectly. This was adopted as standard on the main fleet, replacing the all-over cream that had been in force since 1950. All except the Devon fleet, which retained the cream but with the new logo. The reason for this was that the main competitor in Devon was the BET coaching subsidiary of the Devon General bus company, called Grey Cars! Anyway, perhaps it was Devon cream…

Above: An absolutely classic view of a 1961 Plaxton-bodied Reliance on a local sightseeing excursion making its way along Scarborough's Marine Drive in July 1968. There's a splendid array of contemporary cars, and the population is still showing a resilience to exposure even at the height of summer. Even when, as Stephen Barber observes, "the sea's a lot calmer than ever it was when I was there". *D. Akrigg*

Below: A 1961 Reliance/Plaxton at Glencoe in all-too-familiar Scottish weather.

Above and below: The Hotel Metropole in Leeds was a popular overnight stay for tours from London on their way to Scotland. It still exists today, albeit now named by some marketing guru as 'The Met', and the road outside is now one-way in the other direction. Two Leopards with Plaxton bodywork demonstrate how coach design had advanced in a mere two years between 1961 and 1963. Mind you, 9907 UG had been to Moscow...

Opposite the company's depot in Columbus Ravine, Scarborough, was a parking area for locally based coaches and those visiting from the West Riding. This March 1967 view features a selection of the fleet, headed by a Duple-bodied Ford.

A strange beast, a Duple Firefly-bodied front-engined Albion Victor (one of two dating from 1964 on hire from dealer Stanley Hughes), which briefly reintroduced some red trim.

The reason for narrow coaches. Look how the driver is leaning out of the window to watch the side.

Above: A typical mid-1960s WA touring coach – Leyland Leopard, Plaxton centre-entrance body with sliding windows. BNW 607C stands outside the Prospect Hotel in Harrogate.

Below: It's all matter of taste, but the Duple Continental family of the mid-1960s was pretty special. Leopard BNW 624C with this body – a one-off for WA – stands in dappled shade outside the Bruntsfield Hotel in Edinburgh. *Gavin Booth*

Above: Traditionally, in the 1960s, the newest coaches operated the tours to Spain that were not contracted out to mainland European operators. Duly, in 1966, the new batch of Plaxton-bodied Reliances were given this work, EUG 893D being seen about to collect passengers at Victoria Coach Station. As WA had no licence, it would work 'on hire' to Royal Blue as far as Southampton to catch the overnight ferry.

Below: Sadly, lovely though they were to behold, the AECs of 1966 were plagued by overheating problems, and this became an all-too-frequent sight, which did nothing to enhance Southall's reputation. *D. Akrigg*

Above: The AECs were taken off Spain and returned to UK work, to reduce the mileage of the tow wagon, and the Spanish work was returned to the previous year's Leopards, as evidenced by BNW 603C entering Vicotria Coach station on 27 August 1966.

Below: One of the 1966 Reliances at Aberystwyth in May 1970. As with most new liveries, this tended not to suit older members of the fleet. *Kenneth Evans*

Above: A 1962 Reliance/Plaxton in the Devon fleet threads its way through Torquay, picking up on the way to Clovelly. Just look at the period petrol pumps – and the fabulous mural! *D. Akrigg*

Below: Bretonside bus station in Plymouth, and a 1964 Leopard/Plaxton head-to-head with the competition, Devon General's Grey Cars fleet. They operated identical excursions and charged identical fares, all with the blessing of authority.

Above: Competition in the raw! Leopard 217 HUM and the frankly scary 'Ford Anglia' back end of a Grey Cars Willowbrook-bodied Reliance fighting it out on the streets of Torquay in 1965.

Below: Tour coaches operating into Torquay were pressed into service on those relatively rare free days to help with the busy excursion programme. Still dressed for its main tour and showing off the soon-to-be-discontinued centre-entrance arrangement, Reliance/Plaxton EUG 900D awaits passengers for an afternoon tour to Ilfracombe in August 1967. *D. Akrigg*

Above: Narrow roads and bridges over Dartmoor saw both WA Devon and Grey Cars operating coaches of 7 foot 6 in. width. Judging by its panels, even this was not narrow enough for Reliance/Plaxton EUG 884D! An extra 2 ½ inches would later be added to the width but, despite declining business, narrow coaches would be a feature well into the 1990s.

Below: A delightful summer view of Devon 1968 Leopard/Plaxton MNW 345F awaiting the return of its passengers. Just look at those pre-aircon roof vents; ever tried opening one with the door shut?

Above: An image that speaks for itself. Enjoy it – the sales office at the harbourside in Torquay.

Below: Sales offices were strategically placed around Torquay, and this is the 'Sherwood' office – part of the hotel of the same name – with immaculate advertising and murals. Blackboards were in use until the end of the excursion operation. The coach is a narrow Reliance/Plaxton of 1959.

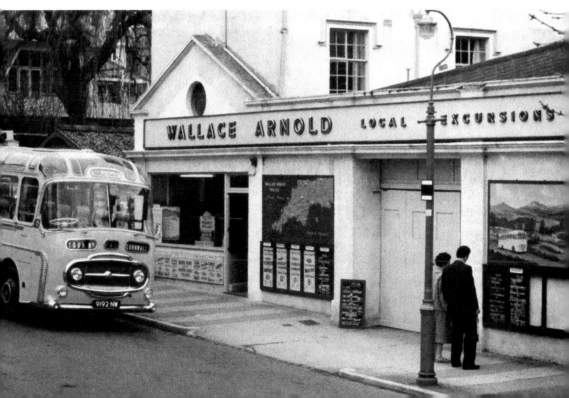

A License to Carry and Prosper

We have touched briefly on the matter of road-service licensing. This was a huge part of WA's work and arguably was a key part in the company's expansion. John King, one-time Managing Director, recalls some court cases taking more than a year to resolve! But in Malcolm Barr WA had an accomplished barrister who knew the ropes and was to be instrumental in a significant coup. From 1957 to 1959 Geoffrey Steel was responsible for licensing at Heap's Tours, a competitor of Wallace Arnold in Leeds; "Think I must have been a thorn in their side," he recalls. He was duly approached by Malcolm Barr and, on 4 January 1960, took over licensing at WA. In the meantime WA had become aware that Heap's was picking up on excursions in Pontefract, something it was not licensed to do, so Malcolm took the trouble to write to proprietor Dennis Heap to assure him that WA knew all about this before Geoffrey joined!

Geoffrey now entered the fray. WA was keen to expand in Scotland, but the state-owned Scottish Bus Group did not share its enthusiasm. In 1962 WA bought the Craiglynne Hotel in Grantown-on-Spey – well known to the company, being used on its tours – and immediately applied for licences to link the main Scottish cities to the hotel, for skiing trips. Despite having no such licences itself SBG objected, then submitted identical applications. The Scottish Traffic Commissioner duly held a Public Inquiry, and Geoffrey found himself in Edinburgh. Proceedings were opened, and the Commissioner announced that he would hear the SBG applications first. Geoffrey objected, pointing out that WA's applications had been submitted first, to which the Commissioner replied that, as it was his Court, he could do as he pleased. There being no objections, the SBG licences were granted as applied for, following which the Commissioner considered the WA applications. These, he announced, were the subject of objections lodged by the SBG, which, moreover, already held identical licences, and were therefore thrown out! Geoffrey was aghast and had to be taken across the road to the Ivanhoe Hotel by one of the SBG team for a calming whisky!

Undeterred, WA really stirred things up the following year by buying up Dickson's of Dundee, which held licences for excursions from that city, and set about building on this with holidays from Edinburgh and Glasgow. SBG fought every inch of the way, and at one hearing WA produced no fewer than forty witnesses to support its application. So fierce was the cross-examination of one witness that she burst into tears, prompting WA's counsel to exclaim: "She only wants to go on holiday!" Geoffrey's suspicion of bias was reinforced when counsel for SBG claimed that "We don't want this English company coming in taking our business." Come in they did though, and under the circumstances the Dickson name was dropped and the WA identity firmly established.

It was reinforced when a link was established with Skye Cars on a weekly ten-hour marathon from Glasgow to Portree, on the Isle of Skye, WA taking it over completely in the mid-1960s. However, the impression of bias continued, and stories abound of highland ferry boats docking at awkward angles to make life difficult for WA drivers.

More peaceful was a major growth in the company's southern catchment area. In something of a coup it took over the tours licences of state-owned bus company United Counties, giving it pick-ups in Luton, Northampton and Bedford, while in 1963 it acquired the goodwill of Hallen Coaches of Bristol, along with Continental tours from that city. The same year brought a very interesting contract to transport staff to and from Fylingdales Early Warning Station, on the North Yorkshire Moors. (Interesting to think that those involved in the front line of the Cuban missile crisis travelled by WA!) There were not many places where WA did not now have a presence, and there's you thinking it was just some coach firm in Leeds.

Perhaps not surprisingly, London was a bit different. Here WA was already one of the big boys, and there was established what became known as the 'String Quartet', comprising London-based Galleon Tours and Glenton Tours, mighty BET company Southdown and WA. This team successfully fought off attempts by others to become established in the capital, and there were often lengthy pitched battles before the Metropolitan Commissioner. There was, however, a side-effect to the String Quartet, for it just as effectively restricted expansion of the constituent members! WA's attempts to get around this led to one of the more spectacular of the company's adventures, to which we will return.

All this activity led to huge growth in the early 1960s. Continental and air passengers doubled in 1963, rising a further 50 per cent the next year. But – and I hope you are gathering this – WA was a company that always tried to anticipate trends, not only in operations but also in the environment in which it ran. With remarkable foresight, in 1964 the company started to computerise its administration, setting up the Northern Computer Bureau (in The Calls), which then sold its services to WA on a time-charge basis. This service was also offered to other businesses in the North of England that were not big enough or did not want their own computer but could benefit from computer time. NCB supplied WA with documentation covering travel tickets, hotel rooming lists, passenger lists, feeder lists and other documents such as agents' statements and internal reports. With a huge administration looking after a myriad pick-up points all over the country and charting offices by now in Leeds, London, Bradford, Hull, Scarborough and Dundee, the company soon felt the benefits of computerisation in a dramatic reduction in administrative work, as did its claimed 'thousands of booking agents'. This was cutting-edge stuff (and, all right, for you computer freaks, the first machine was a Burroughs B383). There was also expansion in the travel-agency side of the business, two of the more notable purchases being in Edinburgh and Leicester.

The growing fleet needed attention too, and a ten-acre site was obtained in 1964 at Gelderd Road in Leeds, on which a new depot was built. This move was also as a result of the success of the car-sales business, which had taken over the old coach depot in Hunslett Road. The new depot opened in October 1966, after coaches had briefly resided in an old Leeds City Transport depot in Donnisthorpe Street, which Chris

Youhill, a driver at the time, remembers as "a horrendous dump". One side-effect of the extra space was that Stanley Hughes would often store coaches at Gelderd Road when they were not on hire to WA. Sometimes they got used...

In 1966 WA was successful in obtaining licences for a tour programme with pick-ups in Preston, Manchester and Liverpool, so a Lancashire programme could be built up at last. But a major development came the following year when the company express services took a dramatic turn. WA started the 'South West Clipper', a network of services linking Yorkshire with coastal resorts, operated by (amongst others) members of the Associated Motorways consortium. Although WA was a minor partner, being responsible for the Friday-night departure from Leeds to the West Country, the company soon realised that this was good work. At 25 pence per mile (in comparison with the 15 pence WA was more used to) the company never turned down the offer of extra work and always gamely volunteered for the longest runs! With the advent of fifty-seven-seaters WA made itself even more indispensable, and there is no doubt the 'Clipper' was a major money-spinner.

Judges of Hastings produced this postcard, already annotated with greetings and good wishes, showing a coach negotiating the Devil's Elbow, near Braemar. This view was often fiddled, but this is a genuine shot of a mid-1950s AEC Reliance/Burlingham Seagull.

Just to show big ones could do it as well, a 1967 Leopard does battle with the Devil's Elbow. It was not unusual for passengers to get out here and walk, but it was always as a driver's 'devilment' rather than any mechanical difficulty.

Above: Watched admiringly by a couple with their Ford Prefect, Leopard 70 BUA makes its way slowly up Lomondside under the control of driver Ernie Warren. With no power steering and a heavy clutch, coupled with a very narrow road, this was not the easiest of journeys. Ernie would go on to become a company legend working in the Traffic Department at Leeds.

Below: The fruits of much of Geoffrey Steel's hard labour! About to head south, a pair of Bedford VALs stand outside the WA office in Sauchiehall Street, Glasgow, early one Saturday in the mid-1960s.

Above: Geoffrey Steel, then WA's Licensing Officer, points proudly at the results of his hard work in the traffic court, getting permission to reduce excursion fares at off-peak times, There had been vociferous objection from fellow licence-holders such as West Yorkshire. It seems incredible now that such a simple thing, so clearly in the public interest, should have been subject to such bureaucracy. Was that what the architects of the 1930 Act intended?

Below: Site preparation at Gelderd Road in 1964. It was a fire clay extraction site and subsidence was a constant problem particularly when an extension to the offices was constructed in the 1990s. The signal box was on the LNWR line from Leeds to Manchester and in railway terms was known as Farnley Junction.

Above: An interesting cross-section of the mid-1960s fleet seen at the end of the decade. Apart from the Bedford VAL (left) all are tour coaches, which normally stayed at Leeds (where the majority of the tour fleet was based). Later in life they would be downgraded, at first to do excursions, express and private hire, before going onto contract work and moving out for their last years to Royston or Castleford depots.

Below: An overview from the mid-1970s showing the Trust Motors Audi/VW showroom. (What price the VW camper vans today?) On the left is the Leeds ring road (now a dual carriageway), while in the foreground is the A62 out of the city. Traffic flow on the depot site was one-way anti-clockwise. Pits were at the front of the building, with three terminal bays and the coach wash farthest away.

Above: The 'South West Clipper' was a joint operation between Yorkshire and South West England involving WA, Yelloway, Yorkshire Traction, Yorkshire Woollen, West Yorkshire, East Midland and members of Associated Motorways – in short, a bunch of old adversaries! This August 1967 view features the arrival of two WAs at the Lymington Road coach park in Torquay. Sensible (or cheeky!) passengers would have travelled in the new Leopard rather than the Bedford VAL, a type somewhat underpowered for such work. Note the lane discipline enforced by upturned tables! *D. Akrigg*

Below: The Kitchin company had a limited licence to Torquay, and the name was kept intact as a group member of the 'Clipper'. This 1968 Reliance/Plaxton – the pride of the fleet, driven by senior driver Bill Buckler – was a regular performer, even to the point of having a specially written blind. It is seen leaving Cheltenham. *D. Akrigg*

More Capital

But what of London? WA was anxious to expand and link into the booming incoming tourist trade, the capital still basking in its 'Swinging London' image. So, in February 1969, WA look over long established Evan Evans Tours. Things could not have been more different. Although the name was well known, particularly to American tourists, and a key office was situated in Russell Square, Evan Evans had no connections with WA or with the base in Croydon and even after purchase was reluctant to help out WA! For starters the fleet was unconventional, to say the least. Of the sixty-one vehicles twenty-three were tiny (twelve-seat) Commer minibuses: at least, it was thought there were twenty-three of them – no one was quite sure. WA soon decided this was a part of the market it could do without.

A classic view of an Evan Evans Duple-bodied Bedford OB in Parliament Square in the 1950s.

Then there were twenty-six quite modern Fords with bodywork by – wait for it – Strachans.

Yes, you heard right. This being a firm not closely associated with building coaches, they had little or no resale value. But there were two magnificent upmarket coaches fitted with every convenience known to man at the time. Surely Evan Evans had got something right then?

They were based on Daimler Roadliner chassis (oh dear!), perhaps the most spectacularly unreliable of an unreliable bunch of rear-engined vehicles. Then there were the totally different working conditions. Much of Evan Evans' work came through contacts with hotel porters and the whole subculture of London hotel life. WA drivers from Leeds were expected to undertake Evan Evans work on their rest days, usually being allocated as the 08.00 spare at Russell Square. Inevitably they got the rougher jobs in contrast with their usual fare. As Francis Elin of Croydon wryly remarks, "They treated them like cavemen." Added to which a booming trade was underway in the middle of the night at the Brandon Road depot selling diesel to cabbies! The WA 1969 annual report states baldly: 'the Evan Evans reorganisation and vehicle replacement proved more expensive than anticipated'. New Bedfords were drafted in, and gradually standards improved, but the outfit was always known to WA staff as 'Evan 'Elp Us'!

Seen near Grosvenor Square is an Evan Evans Bedford SB with bodywork by Thurgood of Ware, a particular favourite. There's also a rather good example of a British Road Services van on the other side of the road, which gives a link, albeit tenuous, with Robert Barr!

Well, they looked the part. WA kept this Ford/Plaxton from the Evan Evans fleet and painted it into the new grey scheme. It is at Gelderd Road awaiting its visit to the paint shop. *G. Pickard*

The Leopard Years

So, there had been great expansion in the coaching side of the business, but none at all on the bus side. In 1967 the Government was muttering darkly about regional transport authorities, and the 1968 Act paved the way for the introduction of Passenger Transport Authorities in the main conurbations. This would clearly have an impact on the Farsley and Kippax operations, WA's 1968 annual report referring to the proposals as 'incompatible with the future growth and development of these companies'. On Saturday 30 March 1968 Farsley Daimler MUB 433 ran in from Rodley to Stannington at 23.15. On the other side of the city, Kippax Leyland PD3 DUG 167C left Leeds bus station at 23.10 for Kippax. Together they marked the end of independently operated services into one of the UK's major cities, which were run with a friendly atmosphere and crews knowing many of their regulars. The following day Leeds City Transport took over, many Farsley staff transferring to its Brantley depot. However, the routes were soon in the hands of one-man-operated AEC Swifts – a portent for WA's remaining bus operation in Scarborough. However, the magnificent LCT Roe-bodied AEC Regent Vs working the Kippax routes were not graced by ex-Kippax staff, none of whom elected to transfer to the distant Torre Road depot. With the exception of two PD3s sent to Scarborough, WA sold all the buses to Stanley Hughes. Six years later LCT would itself be swallowed up by a faceless Passenger Transport Executive.

Another effect of the withdrawal from bus operation in Leeds was that three Alexander-bodied Leyland Panther single-deck buses ordered for Farsley were cancelled. At the time WA had a chief engineer who believed the future lay in rear-engined vehicles (he wasn't alone!) and wanted to order thirty-five Panther coaches. But WA had already seen the problems other operators were having and stuck with the tried and tested Leopard – a wise decision. Had Kippax continued, it would have been re-equipped with Roe-bodied Atlanteans – a type that, in contrast, would have been well at home with LCT. In the event the buses were diverted to Hall's of Hounslow, to work at Heathrow Airport.

As the 1960s drew to a close the whole nature of the WA business was changing. As recently as 1965 coaching had accounted for 80 per cent of the group's profits. But just two years later, with the greater diversification and expansion by the group, this figure was down to 53 per cent.

The 1970s might reasonably be referred to as the Leopard years, for of the decade's 385 new coaches no fewer than 289 were of this type. A few AEC Reliances arrived early on, but the type never recovered, in WA's eyes, from the unreliability of the

1966 batch. Small numbers of Bedfords and Fords came along too, and there were a few interesting additions.

In 1975 six Bristol LHs came for the Devon fleet, the only Bristols ever owned by WA. They had Leyland engines though. Perhaps more dramatic – and a sign of things to come – was the 1971 purchase of a Mercedes-Benz 0302, following a period on loan. Mercedes was astute enough to supply it fully trimmed to WA specification! This was the first WA vehicle to have air suspension – something that would not become commonplace on British coaches for another ten years. The Mercedes was significantly more expensive in terms of the initial purchase price, and WA, in common with most UK operators, stuck to the straightforward Leyland. But it wasn't all straightforward for Leyland. The late Eric Stockwell, who had joined WA as an apprentice in 1950 (his father having been a driver with Bullock's of Featherstone) and went on to become its much respected Chief Engineer, recalls that Leyland deliveries had been unacceptably late in 1971 and that Mercedes had offered to do the whole 1972 order at the Leyland/Plaxton price! Miraculously Leyland delivered the entire 1972 order on time! However, the Leopard was not without its problems, having a tendency to overheat and seize in hot weather. Eric kept a supply of spare engines; "Went on holiday for two weeks, and when I came back all fifteen had gone!" WA believed in getting the most out of its vehicles. The Leeds fleet would arrive at Gelderd Road from tours, and all would be serviced and gone from the depot by 9.30 the following morning. To achieve this WA changed components in advance of their expected life, on the basis that it was better to have a little less value from a part than suffer a breakdown. John King recalls it was a wise policy. On one occasion fifteen coaches had their clutches changed 20,000 miles early to avoid the likelihood of them going during the season, and nine were found to have needed it! As Eric remarked, "An engineering spare is something in a box with the manufacturer's name on it on the shelf." He expected nothing less than perfection.

It is perhaps appropriate here to explain WA's vehicle operating system. This was vehicle-based, the whole season's operations being covered with the maximum utilisation of coaches. Whereas drivers had restrictions on the time they could work, coaches did not, and WA kept them on the move as much as possible. This meant that drivers stayed with their passengers rather than keeping the same coach for, say, a holiday tour. As they arrived at a hotel another driver would appear to whisk away the coach, another miraculously appearing when the first driver next needed one. This was hugely efficient in terms of getting the best return out of the major capital investment. However, as Stephen Barber ruefully reflects, "One cancellation and the whole season's vehicle schedule was up the creek!"

In bodywork terms, WA's close association with Plaxton continued throughout the 1970s, 251 of the vehicles coming from Scarborough. Duple did quite well too, supplying 134, including the whole of the 1976 delivery. To care for the fleet new depots were opened in the 1970s in Torquay and Croydon.

Evan Evans continued to be a headache. The nature of the business made predicting demand difficult. Innovative ideas were tried, for example a sightseeing tour including a hydrofoil trip from the Tower of London to Greenwich, and the Jubilee year of 1977 was the best yet. Although Evan Evans was profitable from 1971, the directors continued to report that its profits were 'not yet satisfactory', and by the end of the decade it would be back in the red.

Things were not too happy either on the day-excursion side in Leeds and Bradford. Despite remaining profitable, they had been in decline since the 1950s, their traditional market being eroded by the car. But even in the mid-1970s WA would often send away ten coaches to Blackpool and Scarborough and on a good day a further ten to Bridlington.

Counter-balancing the decline in excursions was a huge surge in demand for Continental holidays. In 1971 there were 36,000 seats on offer, and a year later this had risen to 42,000. Coach-air holidays were operated using Swissair from Manchester, British Caledonian from Gatwick and Court Line from Luton; from 1972 these were known as WallaceAir. Another name, Aerolink, covered connecting coaches from major Yorkshire cities to Luton and Gatwick, while Scottish customers were fed into Glasgow Airport. Continental trips were not without their particular problems. At first, trains were used from London to the Channel ports, which was fine until there was a rail strike. Francis Flin recalls that delicate financial negotiations had to take place with porters and stewards on the cross-Channel ferries to avoid problems – something that would catch out the unwary! And in this day and age we forget what it was like when communications were more primitive. Francis remembers an AA patrolman calling into a hotel in Welling to advise that the WA coach had been delayed and would arrive late. More spectacular was a coach that broke down in France. The driver no more than walked into a nearby signal-box and asked the signalman to stop the next train to Dijon, which he duly did, and the party were on their way. There was not even a station at the signal-box!

WA continued to develop its core business and gained more picking-up rights in Taunton, Bridgwater, Bristol, Sheffield, Rotherham, Barnsley, Birmingham, Wolverhampton and Coventry, the last three not without a number of objections from West Midlands operators. More vociferous were the objections, twenty-one in all, when the opening of the M62 Trans Pennine motorway prompted WA to seek feeders from Lancashire to its Yorkshire tour programme. Despite the objections' being upheld by the Commissioner, this time WA was not to be put off and successfully appealed to the Environment Secretary. Against opposition from SBG, the Scottish programme expanded, but under a withering burst of objections from twelve operators and British Rail a revolutionary plan for cheap coaches for students to link London with twelve university towns failed. Hardly surprising that, as early as 1974, WA was calling for more freedom in the provision of express coaches. Indeed, the company considered its own brand of upmarket express services, to be known as Motorways, the 'WA' forming the company logo, but believed the returns simply would not have been good enough to offset the cost and trouble of dealing with all the inevitable objections.

The growing Continental market suffered a major setback after the industrial unrest of 1973/4, falling by 50 per cent. There were some spectacular failures, notably Court Line, but WA ensured that not one holiday was lost.

Above: A number of half-cab Daimler CVD6 single-deckers were rebodied by Roe with double-deck bodies and were distinguished by their short rear overhang and unusual stepped rear platform. These features, displayed by LNW 869, can be seen in comparison with a standard Roe product, Leeds City Transport AEC Regent V No. 796, in that operator's distinctive livery.

Below: Although Plaxton was the main supplier of bodywork to the company during the 1960s and into the mid-1970s, WA also took batches of Duple bodies. This delightful scene features a 1972 Duple Viceroy-bodied Leopard pausing at Loch Leven for passengers to enjoy the view.

Above: Tours to Rothesay and Dunoon were a popular feature of the programme throughout the 1960s and 1970s. Until the advent of roll-on, roll-off ferries special short coaches were required for this work, but by 1975 11 metre Leopards such as HWU 63N could use the Gourock–Dunoon ferry, which it is pictured sharing with some splendid cars of the day.

Below: The summer of 1975, with tour coaches loading in the terminal bays at Gelderd Road; Duple, represented by Leopard HWU 77N, was making a comeback and would go on to supply most of the company's new vehicles over the next three years. Bedford YRQ/Plaxton JWX 94N was one of the few lightweights of the time.

Above: Leopard days in 1974, with Spanish regular TUB 1M bringing a little colour to a sea of National white in Victoria Coach Station. *D. Akrigg*

Below: In 1975 WA provided coaches for the Australian and New Zealand rugby teams as well as for Leeds' own. The coaches now look dated, but what about the fashions!

The EU Beckons

John King recalls that WA was a company that tried to anticipate trends, and it correctly predicted that demand for travel across Europe would grow again. Air fares were very high, so WA started express rail holidays to Spain and Italy. However, with the growing importance of the EEC, WA saw the opportunity for direct coach services. Plans were made in 1975 for a London–Rome service, and an international licence was granted in the UK. However, negotiations had to take place with all countries, including France, where the coach was only passing through. The price of agreement was involvement, and WA made arrangements with operators in Paris and Florence, although that did confer picking-up rights. Geoffrey Steel remembers a trial run on the service: "We arrived at the French/Italian border near Chamonix at 02.00 in a blizzard. The Italian border guard insisted on seeing the licence and then disappeared for ages to photocopy it!" Things didn't get any easier. "On arriving in Rome we found tanks on the street. Our joint operators were concerned about our coach so insisted we went to their depot and changed it for one of theirs so it didn't stand out. I enjoyed reading daily orders in Italian!" After all the EEC bureaucracy the service finally got underway in 1977 using an ordinary Leopard/Duple, NNW 100P, for the thirty-seven-hour run. A driver, one Freddie Broadbent, who lived in Milan took over the coach for the final leg to Rome. Being a local, as it were, he soon developed his own style of dealing with border guards so that the coach was not delayed! WA formed a new subsidiary, Euroways Express Coaches, to develop this market, and the Croydon staff uncomfortably shared a kiosk in Victoria Coach Station with arch competitor Magic Bus! Services expanded to Paris and Barcelona, while consideration was given to Vienna and Istanbul. The Moscow Olympics gave WA the spur to explore introducing a service there, and in 1978 the city saw its second WA coach, on a test run, this time a Volvo but still with Plaxton bodywork. An agreement with state-owned National Travel brought operation of services to France, Spain, Italy, Denmark and Greece, and a European variant of the American Greyhound network seemed a distinct possibility. A useful sideline was the – how shall we put it? – 'export' of goods, and a trade in Persian rugs to Spain flourished! Allegedly.

WA also looked at the type of coach for this arduous work. Mercedes-Benz, DAF, Setra and Leyland-DAB were considered for left-hand-drive coaches, but 12-metre Volvos with Plaxton bodywork (featuring fifty-one reclining seats) were bought in 1979; ultimately WA found it easier generally to subcontract this work to other operators. This was not WA's first experience of Volvos, six having been bought in

1978. The B58 was everything the Leopard was, but more powerful. One year was enough, and to Leyland's horror the 1979 order was split almost evenly with Volvo. The writing was on the wall.

Despite all the activity WA remained a family firm. David Kat, who worked in various posts in the 1970s and 1980s, recalls many for whom it was a job for life and who had never worked for anyone else. For full-time staff work maintaining the buildings was found during the quiet winter months. The personal touch was maintained by the traffic office use of three or four staff to operate a manual system of driver allocation. Geoffrey Steel remembers Albert Hartley, Traffic Manager in the late 1950s, who would take a back-up board of the daily orders home with him. First thing in the morning he would prop the board up on his bed and, using the bedside phone (a rare luxury in those days) check that all the drivers were in! But a manual system was not without its pitfalls. David Kat recalls from his time there one occasion when he sent a coach to Hawick instead of Harwich; "If only people could write clearly!" Peter Holt also spent some time in the Traffic Office and recalls boredom in winter and constant mayhem in the summer. On one occasion The Calls telephoned querying a coach Peter had hired in from a local operator. "Do you realise the owner is a farmer and only does coaching in his spare time?" "So what?" "The boot's full of straw bales – there's no room for luggage." The straw overnighted at The Calls. Such was the variety of work covered that spare drivers who had no allocated duty were routinely told to "bring an overnight case with you".

On the bus side double-deck and conductor operation came to an end at Hardwicks when the bus fleet was replaced by four relatively new Park Royal-bodied AEC Swifts acquired in 1971 from Sheffield Transport. Handsome, low-floor (in the context of the time) and one-man-operable they may have been; reliable they were not, and after three years they were replaced by standard Leopards (refitted with bus seats) that had racked up a little too much tour mileage for their bus grant!

Expansion by acquisition slowed considerably in the 1970s, only one company being bought, Embankment Motors of Plymouth, in 1974. The modern fleet of twenty-five Bedfords briefly kept its own identity before being absorbed into the main Devon operation. A milestone was passed in 1976 when the group's profits exceeded £1 million for the first time. By the end of the 1970s WA's 300 coaches were covering more than 10 million miles a year and carrying 2.5 million people. Robert Barr would surely have approved.

Above: WA had sent coaches to Europe from the 1930s, and this tradition continued until the 1960s, when the company realised it was easier to contract the Continental bit to local operators. A major supplier was the West Belgium Coach Company, one of whose Neoplans is seen with Wallace Arnold nameboards attached.

Below: The first Volvos arrived in 1978, although initial discussions had taken place in 1973, the year imports of the B58 chassis began in earnest. A close working relationship with Park's of Hamilton also meant that WA had experience of running the type on hire. By the 1970s Leyland's deliveries were becoming erratic, and its attitude arrogant and inflexible. This was instrumental in the purchase of this vehicle, a great improvement on the ageing Leopard. Despite all this, the company kept faith by splitting its order for 1979 between the two suppliers, but subsequent antics by Leyland helped ensure that Volvo held sway for WA's final twenty years.

Above: Tours by air tended to be met by local coaches, and here a local operator has met a tour that has flown into Milan airport. Seen in Florence in August 1980, the rather plain-looking coach carries a Wallace Arnold nameboard on a livery not too dissimilar to WA's own!

Below: The impressive Dornoch Hotel forms the backdrop for this 1979 Leopard with Plaxton Supreme IV bodywork.

Above: WA's only acquisition in the 1970s was of Embankment Tours of Plymouth in 1974, bringing with it tours and excursions licences from that city. It also brought a fleet of twenty-five Bedford coaches, of which one of the newest, YRQ/Duple UDR 323L, is seen in December 1975 in company with Bristol LH6L/ Plaxton HWU 87N, one of the only six Bristols ever bought by WA – in 1974, when Leyland would not provide short Leopards. David Braund, Engineer in Devon, referred to the LHs as "an absolute nightmare – I towed in more Bristols than Leopards, and there were only six of them!" Fitted with Telma retarders, they would stop rather quickly, drivers suggesting that the chassis stopped before the body! Both coaches seen here carry Embankment fleetnames, but it was subsequently absorbed into the Devon fleet. (Kenneth Evans)

Below: One-man operation was introduced at Hardwick's in 1971 using four Park Royal-bodied AEC Swifts from Sheffield Transport. The latter had gone off rear-engined single-deckers in a big way, altering an order for Bristol REs to one for VRTs. Hardwick's soon found out there was another reason: the things were hideously unreliable. They had a habit of refusing to start at the most embarrassing times, like when full of passengers. Pity – they were stylish buses. They should have been four consecutively numbered vehicles, 20–23, but when the WA drivers arrived to pick them up one of the intended quartet wouldn't start. So they took No. 28 instead! (Geoff Mills)

The End (Part One) –
A Combination of Things

During the 1970s things began to go awry, as they did for many operators. Cost control was not as strong, and standards began to slip. Hotels were not to the standard they had been; Geoffrey Steel particularly recalls one in Den Haag which was renowned throughout WA for always serving meatballs with mustard sauce!

Perhaps the times are best described by two very significant events. The first involved Leyland Vehicles. There is no doubt the Leopard had been a fine machine, but it went well beyond its sell-by date. Wrestling with the dire problems forced upon it by the Government-inspired amalgamation of the company with the out-of-control BMC car group, Leyland quite simply took its eye off the bus and coach ball. By the late 1970s a Leopard replacement was long overdue, and, finally, the Tiger began to take shape. Eric Stockwell claimed that in the Leopard years WA was Leyland's flagship independent customer. As such, it undertook a lot of development work on the Tiger. An early testbed for the Tiger had no provision for the air cleaner, so Eric suggested it had to go where it was fixed on a standard Leopard – there was nowhere else. There it went, and there it stayed. This coach, Leopard/Duple XWX 194S, was, in the words of David Kat, "to be avoided – it wouldn't pull the skin off a rice pudding". A batch of Volvos had trouble with their Wilson gearboxes, fitted to be compatible with WA's Leopard fleet – "failures all over Europe," remembers Eric – so WA decided to order a large fleet of Tigers for 1981. Leyland couldn't oblige and offered Leopards; worse still, Leopards with a type of fuel pump WA had refused before. Nevertheless, worried by the Volvo gearbox failures, WA took thirty-eight Leopards, ironically its largest-ever Leyland order. To add insult to injury, at the big fanfare Tiger launch in Morocco, no WA vehicle was represented. Finally, late in 1981, three Tigers did arrive, but, in its own way, each was to the wrong specification, and WA fell out with Leyland, returning to Volvo. No more Leylands were bought, bringing to an end an association that had lasted since 1925. A sad time indeed.

The other significant development came in 1980 with the advent of British Coachways. A child of the deregulation of coach services, this was a consortium of a number of leading coach operators, the idea being to break the monopoly of state-owned National Express. Although blessed with a large budget, which it spent furiously, British Coachways was doomed from the start, being an uneasy alliance of operators that were often competitors and which had different aims and aspirations. Its terminal facilities, particularly in London, were inferior, and, frankly, the spirited response by National Express was not expected. WA painted three new coaches in British Coachways livery but kept a close eye on things and withdrew after twelve months. Other members did likewise. However, it was a significant episode in British coaching history. Just how much it spurred on National Express will probably never be known, but it certainly influenced one of your authors, then in the state sector, into introducing and heavily publicising new express services himself! However, its relevance to our story is that, drawing upon the experience gained, WA introduced its own 'Pullman' express service from Leeds to London in 1981, initially with high-specification Leopards but subsequently using Bovas with videos and hostesses. In July 1982 this was incorporated into the National Express Rapide network, the coaches donning this livery. WA involvement would continue until 1985.

The early 1980s was characterised by yet more initiatives. The European network, rebranded in 1985 as Euroways, continued to expand, finally being sold in 1989 to National Express. Coach and cruise holidays linking in with P&O's liners *Canberra* and *Oriana* were started in 1980, and the same time, a unique product, InTent, was launched to provide camping holidays to motorists. No-smoking tours were introduced from 1980 (the whole programme went this way in 1991) and, in 1983, in an attempt to capture the youth market, a 'Go Bananas' programme was introduced, a specially liveried Bova helping extol the virtues of drink, discos and nudist beaches at seven European destinations! Meanwhile a new depot for Evan Evans, holding fifty-four coaches, was opened in York Way in 1981, and a 60 per cent stake was taken in the Regency Carriage Company, a London chauffeur-car business.

But underneath all was not well. Although the coach-tour market remained healthy there was strong competition, most notably from National Holidays, which was enjoying significant success in clawing back market share. WA had expected the 1980 deregulation of coach services to be a change for the better and that it would give the company a boost. It did not turn out that way. WA watched as state-owned National Holidays grew at its expense, an experience not helped by the fact that three of the key figures at NH were ex-WA and were using their experience to compete very successfully and thus damage WA's profitability. Many of the company's initiatives did not bring returns as quickly as were needed, and WA was ruthless in shutting them down. InTent was sold in 1984, and Go Bananas only lasted one season. The ground-breaking computer service was also sold in 1984. Operational economies were also undertaken; garages in Castleford, Royston, Pudsey and Bradford were all sold by the early 1980s, all vehicles being based thereafter in Leeds.

The economies were necessary. The late Andy Oxley remembered his days at Castleford: "Away from the pomp of Gelderd Road we were very much left to our own resources, doing contracts for John Smith's brewery, Dunsford & Wesley clothing factory, Dennis Fisher toys at Thorp Arch, Sherburn High School, local schools to Kippax baths, working men's clubs to the coast, excursions, trips to Elland Road dogs and a lot of Clipper work at weekends."

A very clear example of the type of work likely to be encountered in the area at that time. Generally drivers were allocated their own coach, and Andy well remembered his Leopard/ Plaxton, EUG 444K, which, unlike other members of the batch, had a four-spoke steering wheel rather than the two-spoke that was by then standard. Andy remembered them as happy days. But the Dunsford & Wesley and Fisher Toys contracts ended, and closure became inevitable. Few of the staff transferred to Leeds.

In 1983 WA finally gave up on Evan Evans, selling it for a mere £40,000 to the Insight group – not a very cheerful end to what had been a troubled adventure. The Fylingdales contract, which was by now using the oldest vehicles, ended in 1985, and in the same year the Croydon garage was closed, coach servicing moving to the London Buses garage at Norwood.

As for coaches, the Volvo B10M/Plaxton combination was favoured, although a fleet of twenty-nine Bovas and six Setras was built up in 1982/3. Eric Stockwell recalled the Setras as having big rear engines and syncromesh gearboxes. Rev counters were provided to indicate when gear-changes were necessary, but, as Eric put it, "Being used to changing gear by engine noise, drivers didn't understand how to drive them." With increasing choice it was proposed to buy small batches of Volvos, DAFs, Leyland Royal Tiger Doyens, Setras and Bovas (two types) to try them out. But, with the structure of the coach market changing, this just seems to epitomise the company's apparent loss of direction.

Three coaches were painted in British Coachways livery from the off in 1980 so that WA could be seen as leaders in the club. They were pretty much leaders on the way out too. Not unattractive, the livery was deliberately copied from British Airways. *Andrew Jarosz*

Above: After British Coachways, in 1981 WA tried a Leeds–London 'Pullman' service. Here Leopard/Plaxton PNW 296W passes Leeds bus station on its way to The Calls. *Andrew Jarosz*

Below: Finally the Pullman became part of the National Express Rapide network. Here Bova Europa VWX 370X passes Lord's Cricket Ground in October 1983, in full Rapide livery. This was beyond the pale for the Barr family, and the contract was terminated in 1985. *Kevin Lane*

Above: The 'Go Bananas' product was aimed at the Club 18–30 market, emphasised by this cleverly painted Bova Europa. The concept was not a success, and the coach later reverted to a more genteel appearance.

Below: For three days in 1982 nearly fifty travel staff, invited by the English Tourist Board, explored Northumbria, staying at the four-star Gosforth Park Hotel. They visited Hexham, Hadrian's Wall, Alnwick and Holy Island, were welcomed by Lord Armstrong to lunch at Bamburgh Castle and enjoyed a medieval banquet at Lumley Castle. Transport was provided by one of WA's brand-new Setra touring coaches. It was called an 'educational'.

Glory Days (Part Two) – The Cavalry

What was to be done? Malcolm Barr was not prepared to sit back and watch the family firm go into terminal decline. In the turbulent days of 1985, when the greater challenge of bus deregulation was looming, he went out and recruited the entire National Holidays management team! This brought back, amongst others, John King (as Managing Director) and Stephen Barber (initially as Operations Director), both of whom had been with the company during the 1960s and 1970s. Immediately they sat down to work out how to turn things around.

The new team set out new policies. The first thing was the fleet. Eric Stockwell, highly regarded for his down-to-earth views on coaches, was consulted. He was in no doubt that the Volvo/Plaxton combination was a winner, so previous indications of intent were rescinded, and Volvo/Plaxtons became the standard.

Peter Holt recalls a conversation with Stephen Barber many years before. Stephen's view was that WA should get its core business – tours – 100 per cent correct, then look at other products. The new team after 1985 did just that, putting a lot of investment into high-specification coaches, aiming at the older end of the market and giving, at considerable cost, the company's 7,000 booking agents a highly efficient booking system. They wanted to provide the country's most modern fleet and decided on a three-year vehicle life. They also embarked upon a policy of 'contracting out the livery', whereby operators provided coaches in WA livery to work within their own areas, such distinguished names as Southdown and East Yorkshire signing up. Shades of National Holidays! However, the same personalities were still to be found. One summer four regular drivers were used for the Ilfracombe tour. The first to arrive promptly got a job as a deck-chair attendant on the beach. As each driver arrived during the season, he duly took over these duties. At the height of summer, all four found themselves in the resort together and decided to have a few drinks. As is the way with UK weather, when they were in the pub, a sudden storm whipped up. All the deck-chairs were washed out to sea, and the 'attendant' (all four of him) was duly sacked!

In 1986 the company once again tried coastal express services, but this attempt just confirmed its view that it was a holiday company running coaches, and decided to stick with that. Where they fitted in with the core business, excursions and private hires were taken on.

Also in 1986 the more dramatic deregulation of buses had taken place. The Harwick's operation in Scarborough initially took advantage of this, extending the bus route and taking on tendered services using Leyland Nationals, while two more double-deckers, this time of the ubiquitous ex-Greater Manchester Atlantean type, were converted to open-top for a seafront service. But after twelve months of deregulated operation the team realised, again, that concentrating on their core activity was the way forward. The excursion market in Scarborough had also changed dramatically, and in 1987 the whole operation was sold to East Yorkshire.

From 1987 the significant Cotter Group of Glasgow began a rapid decline, and WA picked up some of the firm's English operations before, in October 1987, taking over the whole group. Gradual integration of the business, under the Cotter name but in WA house style, took place in Scotland over the next three years. In 1988 the four main coach holiday programmes of the International Leisure Group were taken over. In the same year, as a measure of the success of the new regime, WA was voted Top Coach Holiday Operator by the 6,500 travel agents polled by the well-regarded *Travel Trade Gazette*. It won again in 1989, and by 1990 was the second-largest coach-tour operator in Britain, carrying some 250,000 people a year. WA, affectionately known as 'Wally's Trollies', had become a British institution.

WA stuck with Volvo for chassis, but, with shades of times past, this was not without its dramas. Soon the company was seen as a leading customer and was an important guest at the launch of the Mark III B10M in Stockholm. Amid the dry ice after the spectacular launch a Volvo executive asked Eric Stockwell, who had been closely examining the new product, what he thought of it. "It's crap!" said Eric, and he proceeded to explain why. With all due credit to Volvo, six months later a senior representative rang Eric to say he'd been absolutely right!

Things were not quite the same with Plaxton, which WA had continued to patronise. When, in 1991, it launched a whole new range, the company ordered sixty-one coaches off the drawing board for the 1992 season. They proved a nightmare, some coaches leaking so badly that duckboards had to be placed in the luggage lockers to keep passengers' cases dry. The next year WA took but five Plaxtons and started a very successful arrangement with foreign coachbuilders Van Hool and Jonckheere. Stephen Barber recalls that Van Hool built the whole order in line. When the first one was complete he and Eric Stockwell were invited over to Belgium to make sure it was as specified. On one occasion some minor modifications were found to be necessary, and on returning from lunch, Stephen found that the required adjustments had been made to every coach in the order! Nevertheless, by 1995 WA had returned to the Volvo/Plaxton combination.

Malcolm Barr still had the entrepreneurial spirit that so epitomised WA. When rail privatisation came along, he was very keen, but not in whole franchises. For instance he wanted to run the 'Flying Scotsman' – not all the East Coast, just that bit. In those early days the Strategic Rail Authority was not averse to such approaches. He also wanted to buy a small airline, believing that WA's strict vehicle operations, when applied to planes, could drastically reduce costs. But these ideas came to nothing.

Increasingly, WA concentrated on providing its own coaches for Continental operations, and if Eurostar or SNCF TGV express trains were used for part of the journey, usually there was a WA coach waiting at the other end. More industry awards followed. The new policies seemed to be delivering. To cap it all, celebrations in 1996 to mark seventy years of operation saw gala dinners on a number of the company's tours and a special seventieth-anniversary Round Britain fifteen-day tour, yours for £599.

All in all, the new team could rightly feel that they had continued the vision set by Robert Barr those seventy years ago.

This just sums up a coach-tour holiday. You get taken to somewhere spectacular, then stop so you can enjoy it. This superb picture from April 1986 shows Chesil Beach (Dorset) stretching right back to Portland – a stunning view being enjoyed by the passengers of Leopard/Plaxton EBW 36A. This registration had originally graced a 1985 Volvo/Plaxton – a situation the new management found illogical, hence its transfer to an older Leyland, formerly PNW 299W. *Kenneth Evans*

Last of the narrow vehicles were a batch of 1970s Leopards rebodied with the dinky Plaxton bodies and registered in 1986. Seen leaving Bristol's Marlborough Street bus station, then home to some odd badgers, CSU 936 will have encountered few narrow bridges on its way up the M5.

Above: Extensive hiring was standard practice for WA, and in later years other operators' coaches appeared in WA colours. A long-term provider was Park's of Hamilton, a company that seemed willing to try anything! Here a WA-liveried Bova/Duple Calypso integral (a type described unkindly by some as a 'Collapso'), with DAF engine, of 1984 is seen amongst more traditional WA fare at Gelderd Road.

Below: In a move unimaginable in National Bus Company days, Brighton-based Southdown painted several coaches in WA livery in 1987. Here Southdown Leyland Tiger 1004, complete with cherished registration from a 'Queen Mary' PD3, is seen in Chester – a sight that would have former BET men spinning in their graves! *Brian Peters*

Above: Another of Park's remarkable vehicles to appear in WA livery was this DAF SBR3000 with Plaxton Paramount 4000 body capable of carrying seventy-four people and still with space for a washroom and ample luggage. It provided the largest capacity WA had ever used and worked shuttles to Spain in 1987.

Below: East Yorkshire was another former competitor to provide vehicles for WA following NBC privatisation. This 1988 photgraph shows one of its Leyland Royal Tiger Doyens in a version of WA livery. So a Doyen did finally appear in WA livery after the bust-up in the early 1980s.

Above: The increase in bus work brought with it two second-hand Leyland Nationals from Greater Manchester Buses. This one shows well the 'whirling wheel' British Leyland symbol. After a year of deregulation the whole Hardwick's operation was sold to East Yorkshire, which absorbed it into its Scarborough & District fleet. Although widespread in the UK, the National was uncommon in both fleets. *Andrew Jarosz*

Below: In 1973 six Leopards were bought with bus doors to qualify for bus grant. They came perilously close to running up too much mileage on tours to justify their grant, so, just in time, they were fitted with bus seats to replace the unreliable Swifts at Hardwick's. Two birds with one stone really. PNW 312W, one of the 1981 Leopard replacements converted from a standard tour coach, is seen working the post-deregulation extension of the bus route to Helmsley – deep in what had been United territory – behind one of Scarborough & District's 'Scarborough Skipper' minibuses. *John Marsh*

Above: The last two buses were bought for marketing rather than service work. They were ex-Southdown Northern Counties-bodied Leyland PD3 open-toppers of the famous 'Queen Mary' style. One, seen here, was *Uncle Wally*, formerly Southdown 425, based at Leeds; the other was *Uncle Arnold* in Torquay. *Andrew Jarosz*

Below: Many leading companies fell by the wayside in the 1980s once they lost the protection of licensing. WA took the opportunity to purchase a number of such companies, employing joint branding in an attempt to extract the last vestiges of customer goodwill from an old respected name. One such was Bee-Line of Middlesbrough, and this 1985 Volvo/Plaxton, with cherished 'WA' registration, shows the outcome. *Brian Peers*

Above: In 1987, WA bought two of Volvo's rather racy C10M coaches, which were distinguished by their long wheelbase and hefty price tag, being almost £20,000 more than a standard Volvo/Plaxton. Both were used extensively on mainland Europe, the second being seen in St Anton on an Alpine tour.

Below: The Cumbria Grand in genteel Grange-over-Sands was a popular destination. Here a 1989 Volvo B10M/Plaxton Paramount loads its customers for a local tour of the nearby Lake District. *Tony Greaves*

Above: Dodsworth's Coaches – 'if in difficulty, ask Doddy' – of Boroughbridge was a regular supplier to WA for more than forty years, and some coaches, like this neat Plaxton-bodied Scania K93, wore the livery for a while.

Below: More usual fare from Park's of Hamilton: a Plaxton-bodied Volvo B10M at Gelderd Road in 1991.

Above: Also providing liveried coaches in the early 1990s was Premier Travel of Cambridge, one of whose Plaxton-bodied Volvo B10Ms is seen at WA's South Mimms interchange.

Below: Doncaster-based Travelgreen – a name to die for in the twenty-first century – was a major provider of minicoaches for tour feeder work. This smart Mercedes was turned out in WA livery.

Above: One of five Plaxton-bodied Mercedes O303s purchased in 1990 leaves the Gelderd Road terminal. *Andrew Jarosz*

Below: Plaxton became WA's major body supplier (it was and remains based in Scarborough) from 1958, when a strike at the Duple factory resulted in twenty Reliances' being sent to them for bodying. By 1990 Plaxton had supplied WA with more than 1,000 bodies, and to mark this significant milestone a replica model was presented to the company. At the celebrations are (from left to right) WA Deputy Chairman Stuart Barr, Chairman Malcolm Barr. David Matthews (Chairman and Chief Executive of Plaxton) and Colin Cowdery (Managing Director, Plaxton Sales)

Above: A convoy of new Volvo coaches prepare to leave the Plaxton factory in Scarborough in 1991. *Ray Mantell*

Below: Volvo J701 CWT, on tour near Balmoral in April 1994, was one of those off-the-drawing-board Plaxton Premieres. Good job it wasn't raining, bearing in mind the early problems with this design. *Kenneth Evans*

Above: The 1993 influx of Van Hool and Jonckheere bodies arriving in Leeds.

Below: A commercially published postcard. The coach, a 1994 Volvo B10M Excalibur, on tour 1336L, is approaching the Devil's Elbow to reach the top of the Cairnwell Pass between Glen Shee and Braemar. The driver, Tony Richardson, formerly with one of the other members of the 'String Quartet', Glenton Tours, reported that this tour was as near perfect as any he had operated over forty years and that the clients loved it!

En route to Sorrento and Capri, a 1993 Volvo/Van Hool pauses outside the Vatican in St Peter's Square, Rome.

WA had an exclusive moquette produced by Holdsworth's of Halifax. This is the interior of a 1993 Van Hool-bodied Volvo B10M purchased in the wake of the Plaxton problems.

Above: By 1994 Continental tours were operated by the company's own coaches equipped with air-conditioning. Two batches of Van Hool-bodied Volvos were brought in 1993/4 and formed the backbone of the mainland European tour fleet. This one is seen in Paris.

Below: A successful homecoming for Castleford Rugby Club in 1986. An open top tour of the streets was deemed necessary, and until the advent of the ex-Southdown open-toppers, one had to be borrowed, this PD2 coming from Lancaster. *Malcolm King*

Above: Huddersfield Town was another club transported by WA in the 1980s and 1990s, the team coach, a Volvo B0M/Plaxton Premiere complete with cherished 'WA' plates, being seen at Wembley in 1994.

Below: The Australian Rugby League team used a WA coach from the 1950s, although the vehicle provided in those days would have borne little resemblance to this magnificent machine, supplied for the 1994 tour. Fitted with Jonckheere bodywork, L965 NWW was WA's only three-axle Volvo B12.

Above: In 1992 a special high-specification coach designed in association with the club was bought for Leeds United, appearing at that year's Bus & Coach Show. A B10M/Plaxton Excalibur, it is seen outside Newcastle United's ground with the (sadly) necessary police protection.

Below: Leeds Rhinos Rugby League club was a long-standing customer. Here the team coach, a Plaxton-bodied Volvo, passes Cardiff Market, an emporium of the same standing as Kirkgate Markets in Leeds, on its way to the Millennium Stadium. The locals seem quite welcoming, despite this being the wrong type of rugby.

Above: In Dublin's fair city is N224 HWX, a 1995 Plaxton Premiere 350-bodied Volvo B10M. The snags with this style had by now been ironed out, and WA had resumed placing large orders. On the right is one of Dublin's weird Bombardier double-deckers.

Below: Tours to Ireland were always popular, but the political troubles of the 1970s had a detrimental effect on patronage. More stable times resulted in WA's providing a much-enlarged programme, and six coaches are here parked in Dublin in 1996 whilst their customers spend time sightseeing.

Above: Two batches of Toyota Coaster/Caetano Optimo nineteen-seaters were used for feeder work in the 1990s.

Below: Former buses were often used as a mobile control offices at the various interchange sites. At Medway Services on the M2 this role was performed by a Massey-bodied Atlantean that had started life as a trolleybus replacement with Maidstone Corporation. It was also used to celebrate WA's seventieth anniversary. Note the use of an electric milk float for luggage transfer.

The End (Part Two) – and an Abrupt One Too

In 1997 irreconcilable differences in the Barr family interests led to the sale of the business. Although this was, more happily, to a management buy-out, there was a strong venture-capital backing to make it work. Things continued much as before, and a significant purchase – and an ironic one at that – was National Holidays. Harking back to pre-war days, a new programme of high-quality tours using high-specification coaches in a classy livery was launched under the 'Grand Tourer' banner. This was immediately successful and at last brought a WA coach to Morocco! However, in 2005, the venture-capitalist backers purchased major competitor Shearings and promptly merged the two companies. Apart from a token nod towards the WA identity, to all intents and purposes that is the end of our tale.

The 'Grand Tourer' concept was the final blooming of Wallace Arnold entrepreneurship. Carrying a distinctive livery, these Jonckheere- and Plaxton-bodied Volvos had thirty-six leather seats, and the specification included a rear lounge, an individual sound system and a navigation system that displayed the coach's position – just like a plane! Such was the attention to detail that BMW paints, black and gold, were used, as shown by this Jonckheere-bodied coach.